S0-CFZ-509

PROBLEM SOLVING STRATEGIES

GLOBE FEARON EDUCATIONAL PUBLISHER
A Division of Simon & Schuster
Upper Saddle River, New Jersey

Executive Editor: Barbara Levadi
Editors: Bernice Golden, Lynn Kloss, Bob McIlwaine, Kirsten Richert
Production Manager: Penny Gibson
Production Editor: Walt Niedner
Interior Design: The Wheetley Company
Electronic Page Production: Curriculum Concepts
Cover Design: Pat Smythe

Printed in the United States of America 1 2 3 4 5 6 7 8 9 10 99 98 97 96

ISBN 0-8359-1537-9

GLOBE FEARON EDUCATIONAL PUBLISHER
A Division of Simon & Schuster
Upper Saddle River, New Jersey

CONTENTS

LESSON 1:   The Problem Solving Process **2**

LESSON 2:   Choose an Operation **6**

LESSON 3:   Too Much Information **8**

LESSON 4:   Formulating a Problem **10**

LESSON 5:   Act It Out **12**

LESSON 6:   Guess and Test **14**

LESSON 7:   Use Estimation **16**

LESSON 8:   Work Backward **18**

LESSON 9:   Break a Problem into Smaller Parts **20**

LESSON 10:   Draw a Diagram **22**

LESSON 11:   Use a Table or Graph **24**

LESSON 12:   Make a Table **28**

LESSON 13:   Make an Organized List **30**

LESSON 14:   Find a Pattern **32**

LESSON 15:   Make a Generalization **34**

LESSON 16:   Solve a Simpler Problem **36**

LESSON 17:   Solve Another Way **38**

LESSON 18:   Use a Sample **40**

LESSON 19:   Use Venn Diagrams **42**

LESSON 20:   Use Logical Reasoning **44**

LESSON 21:   Use Critical Thinking **46**

Lesson 22: Find the Break-Even Point **48**

Lesson 23: Write an Equation **50**

Cumulative Review (Lesson 1–4) **52**

Cumulative Review (Lesson 5–9) **53**

Cumulative Review (Lesson 10–13) **54**

Cumulative Review (Lesson 14–17) **55**

Cumulative Review (Lesson 18–21) **56**

Cumulative Review (Lesson 22–23) **57**

Answer Key **58**

TO THE STUDENT

Access to Math is a series of 15 books designed to help you learn new skills and practice these skills in mathematics. You'll learn the steps necessary to solve a range of mathematical problems.

LESSONS HAVE THE FOLLOWING FEATURES:

❖ Lessons are easy to use. Many begin with a sample problem from a real-life experience. After the sample problem is introduced, you are taught step-by-step how to find the answer. Examples show you how to use your skills.

❖ The *Guided Practice* section demonstrates how to solve a problem similar to the sample problem. Answers are given in the first part of the problem to help you find the final answer.

❖ The *Exercises* section gives you the opportunity to practice the skill presented in the lesson.

❖ The *Application* section applies the math skill in a practical or real-life situation. You will learn how to put your knowledge into action by using manipulatives and calculators, and by working problems through with a partner or a group.

Each book ends with *Cumulative Reviews*. These reviews will help you determine if you have learned the skills in the previous lessons. The *Selected Answers* section at the end of each book lists answers to the odd-numbered exercises. Use the answers to check your work.

Working carefully through the exercises in this book will help you understand and appreciate math in your daily life. You'll also gain more confidence in your math skills.

THE PROBLEM SOLVING PROCESS

Shanelle works for the TV quiz show "What's My Number?" She is helping the quizmaster rehearse. The quizmaster asks Shanelle to come up with the greatest number that has the digits 5, 7, and 9. Each digit can be used only once. What is the number?

You can use a four-step process to solve this problem.

Understand the Problem

What do I know?

I know that I can use the digits 5, 7, and 9 once each.

What do I need to find?

The greatest number these digits can form.

Plan

What can I do?

I'll use the greatest digit in the hundreds place, the next-greatest digit in the tens place, and the least digit in the ones place.

Carry out the plan

I'll try my plan.

The greatest digit is 9, 7 is next, and 5 is least. So I get 975.

Look back

Have I answered the question?

Yes, I found the greatest number.

Is the solution reasonable?

To make sure, I'll place 7 in the hundreds place. That gives 795 or 759. Placing 5 in the hundreds place gives 579 or 597.

All are less than 975.

Reminder

To make the least number, use what you know about placing digits for the greatest number. This time, try putting the least digit in the hundreds place.

Solve, using the four-step process. Write the four steps.

1. What is the least number you can make using the digits 3, 4, and 7 only once?

   a. Understand
   What do you know?

   _____

   What do you need to find?

   _____

   b. Plan
   What can you do?

   _____

   c. Carry out
   Try your plan.

   _____

   d. Look back
   Did you answer the question?

   _____

   Does your solution seem reasonable?

   _____

Reminder

You have to do two different things to solve this problem.

2. At the quiz show production company, Anya earned $5.25 per hour after taxes. After she got paid for 10 hours, she paid a bill for $45. How much did she have left?

   a. Understand
   Anya made $5.25 per hour for _____ hours.

   She paid a bill of _____.

   How much did she have left? _____

   b. Plan
   Multiply to find out how much money Anya earned after taxes.

   Subtract the amount of the bill.

   c. Carry out
   What Anya earned: _____

Amount she paid: _____

What she had left: _____

d. Look back

Has the question been answered? _____

Does your answer seem reasonable? Why?

_____

Exercises

Use the four steps you have learned to solve each problem. Write the steps for the first problem.

3. What is the greatest number you can make using any three digits from 1 to 9? A digit may be used no more than two times.

a. Understand _____

b. Plan _____

c. Carry out _____

d. Look back _____

4. What is the least number you can make using three digits from 1 to 9? Each digit may be used *only once*.

_____

5. The quizmaster asks one contestant to think of a number that is greater than twice 30 and less than twice 35. The number has a 6 in the ones place. What is the number?

_____

6. Now the quizmaster asks for two even numbers that contain the digits 6, 7, and 9, used once each. Which *two* numbers is he thinking of?

_____

7. Larome wants to buy a "What's My Number?" jacket for $24. He earns $5 an hour after taxes. How many hours will he have to work to pay for the jacket?

_____

8. Contestants earn 10 points for each right answer and lose 5 points for each wrong answer. Hiroko ended up with 25 points for the first round. She got 4 answers correct. How many did she get wrong?

_____

9. At a buffet lunch after filming the show, Camilla took 6 cookies. She ate 2 and gave the rest to Jenny. Jenny ate 1 and gave the rest to Jack. Jack gave 1 cookie back to Camilla. How many cookies did Jack keep for himself?

_____

Application

Write the steps you use to solve the problems.

10. At a restaurant, four quiz show coworkers have dinner. The bill comes to $37.50. If the four split the bill equally, how much will each pay?

   a. Understand _____

   b. Plan _____

   c. Carry out _____

   a. Look back _____

11. Make up a riddle that uses numbers. Write the riddle and its solution below.

_____

_____

_____

_____

_____

_____

_____

_____

_____

Vocabulary

operation: addition, subtraction, multiplication, or division

Reminder

Use the four-step process to solve problems:
1) understand
2) plan
3) carry out the plan
4) look back

Reminder

You can use more than one operation to solve a problem.

CHOOSE AN OPERATION

Suppose you are planning a four-day vacation. You have $300 to spend. How much can you spend each day?

You can use one of four **operations** to solve this problem: addition, subtraction, multiplication, or division.

To choose an operation, ask yourself these questions:

- **What do I know?** *I know the total amount of money and the number of days I will be on vacation.*

- **What do I need to know?** *I need to know how much money I can spend each day.*

In your mind, picture yourself separating the $300 into four equal amounts. To separate any amount into equal amounts, you can *divide*.

$$\$300 \div 4 = \$75$$

You can spend $75 each day.

To check your answer, use another method.

$$\$75 \times 4 = \$300$$

or

$$\$75 + \$75 + \$75 + \$75 = \$300$$

Guided Practice

1. A museum tour guide counts 63 people waiting for a tour. Then 5 people leave and 8 more enter. How many people are there now?

   To find out how many people there are, subtract the 5 who left:

   $63 - 5 = $ _____ people

   Then add that number to the number of people who entered:

   _____ $+ 8 = $ _____ people in all

Choose the correct operation or operations. Then solve.

2. Rochelle is budgeting $50 for each day of her vacation. She will be on vacation for one week. How much is she planning to spend?

_____

3. A group of 7 tourists plans to make dinner reservations at a restaurant. Then 2 people say they can't come. After that, 3 other people ask to join the group. How many people will be in the dinner group?

_____

4. The tour leader puts out 4 rows of chairs. She puts 7 chairs in 3 of the rows but has only 6 chairs for the last row. How many people can she seat?

_____

Application

 Use a calculator to help you solve these problems.

5. Plan a weekend trip. Figure how much you would spend getting there by car, bus, train, or plane. Find out how much it costs to stay overnight at a motel, hotel, or campground. Estimate how much you would spend on food each day. How much money would you need?

_____

_____

6. Write a problem that can be solved using one or more operations. Solve the problem and explain the solution.

_____

_____

_____

_____

_____

_____

TOO MUCH INFORMATION

Vocabulary

cost: the price of something

profit: the amount left over after all the costs have been paid

Reminder

You may use more than one operation to solve a problem.

Sometimes a problem has too much information. To solve this kind of problem, you must concentrate on the information that is necessary to solve the problem. Ignore the extra information.

Follow the steps to solve the problem below.

A clothing store manager buys 10 shirts for $20 each. She plans to sell the shirts for $30 each. The customer will pay a sales tax of 5% on each shirt. What is the store's profit on each shirt?

Step 1
Identify the information you need to solve the problem.
I need to know how much each shirt costs the store.
I need to know what the store charges for a shirt.
I **don't** need to know the sales tax.

Step 2
Write down what you know.
How much does the store pay for each shirt?
How much does the store sell the shirt for?

Step 3
Use this information to solve the problem.
$30 − $20 = $10

The store's profit is $10 on each shirt.

Guided Practice

1. Miguel bought a bike for $50. His sister bought a bike for $10 more. Miguel spent $30 fixing up his bike, and then sold it for $100. What was his profit?

   Necessary information: What the bike cost, what Miguel paid to fix it up, and what he sold it for.

   Unnecessary information: What his sister paid.

   Solution: Miguel's cost: $50 + $30 = $80

   Miguel's profit: $100 − $80 = _____

Exercises

Identify the necessary information. Then solve the problem. Use a calculator to help you.

2. A compact disc costs $11.99 at Surf City Music Store and $14.99 at Elsa's Music. Yaron bought 3 compact discs at Surf City. How much did he spend?

Necessary information:

_____

Solution:

_____

3. The assistant buyer at Bell Shoes buys 100 pairs of shoes for $4,000 to sell this month. The store will sell each pair for $75. Next year the store plans to raise the price for shoes to $85 per pair. What is the store's profit on the shoes that were just bought if all are sold?

Necessary information:

_____

Solution:

_____

Application

COOPERATIVE LEARNING Work with a partner to solve the following problem. Explain how you solved it. Then work together to write your own problem with extra information.

4. A certain job pays $5.00 an hour. You can work 2 days a week for 8 hours each day. Lunch costs about $4.00 a day, and the bus fare is $1.25 each way. For this job, how much will your expenses be each week?

_____

_____

5. Write your own problem. Give it to another pair to solve.

_____

_____

FORMULATING A PROBLEM

Look at the advertisement below. What problems could you write that could be answered using the information given in the ad?

To write a problem, ask a question. For example:
How much more does one game cost than another?
How much do 4 copies of the same game cost?
How much money will you save?

Then turn your question into a math problem.

Suppose your question is:
How much more does Share Racer cost than Reach the Beach?

To find the answer, write a subtraction sentence.

$$\$59.99 - \$51.99 = ?$$

Then use a calculator to solve.

$$\$59.99 - \$51.99 = \$8.00$$

Share Racer costs $8.00 more than Reach the Beach.

Guided Practice

1. Try writing and solving another problem that uses a different operation.

   Problem: How much will _____ copies of Wild World cost at the sale price?

   Multiplication sentence: _____ $\times$ $28.79 = ?

   Solution: _____ $\times$ $28.79 = _____

Exercises

Use the video game ad. Write four problems: addition, subtraction, multiplication, and division. Then solve the problems, using a calculator when necessary.

2. Problem:

_____

_____

Solution:

_____

3. Problem:

_____

_____

Solution:

_____

4. Problem:

_____

_____

Solution:

_____

5. Problem:

_____

_____

Solution:

_____

Application

6. Find a price list in a catalog or advertisement. Write and solve two problems that can be answered using the price list.

_____

_____

_____

ACT IT OUT

To solve a problem, you can use **manipulatives** to "act it out." In some problems, the numbers are small but the process is hard to keep track of. Working a problem out with objects keeps you on track.

Manipulatives can help you solve the following problem.

Peter has 7 coins in his pocket. They add up to $1.00. What coins does he have?

Use paper slips or coins. Try this combination.

These 7 coins only add up to $0.77.

Try other combinations until you find one that adds up to $1.00.

The solution is 2 quarters and 5 dimes.

Guided Practice

Here is another type of problem that manipulatives can help you solve.

1. A railroad worker added 2 cars to a 9-car train. At the next stop, a worker took off 5 cars. At the third stop, a worker added 2 cars. How many cars long is the train now?

   Use slips of paper, coins, or paper clips.

   Step 1: Show 9 cars.

   Step 2: Add 2 cars.

   Step 3: Subtract 5 cars.

   Step 4: Add 2 cars.

   How many cars are left? _____

Use manipulatives to solve the following problems.

2. An airline clerk sells 14 tickets for a flight on a small plane. A family of 3 then cancels their tickets. Then 5 vacationers and 2 businessmen book seats. How many people will be traveling on the plane?

_____

3. While waiting for a flight, Greg reads a games magazine. One page contained a challenge: "What coins add up to $0.49? Show the solution using the fewest coins possible." Greg gets the answer right. What was his answer?

_____

4. At the airport, Zac wants to buy a newspaper for $0.85. He has 4 coins in his pocket that add up to exactly the right amount. What 4 coins does he have?

_____

5. An elevator begins a trip at the first floor. The elevator goes up to the 3rd floor. Then it goes up 3 floors, down 3 floors, up 5 floors, and down 7 floors. What floor is the elevator on?

_____

Application

6. Write a problem that can be solved using coins or another manipulative. Give your problem to a partner to solve.

_____

_____

_____

_____

7. How do manipulatives help you solve problems?

_____

_____

_____

GUESS AND TEST

Vocabulary

area: the number of square units needed to cover a region

perimeter: the distance around a figure

Reminder

You can use drawings or manipulatives to solve guess and test problems.

Gwynne has 20 meters of fencing. She wants to enclose the greatest possible area within the fence. What is the greatest **area** for a rectangle with a **perimeter** of 20 meters?

She can use the Guess and Test strategy.

Guess: On graph paper, Gwynne draws a rectangle that is 8 units by 2 units. The perimeter, or distance around the rectangle, is 20 units.

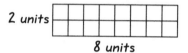

Test her guess: To find the area, or number of square units, she counts the squares in the rectangle. She could also find the area by multiplying the length times the width.

So, 8 units × 2 units = 16 square units.

This rectangle would have an area of 16 sq. m.

Guess again: Then she tries another rectangle.

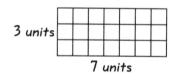

Test: The area is 7 units × 3 units = 21 units.

Its area is greater than the area of the first rectangle.

Guess again, using new information: Since the area got greater when the length and width were closer in size, Gwynne tries a 5-unit by 5-unit rectangle.

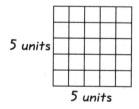

Reminder

To find the area, multiply the length times the width. To find the perimeter, find the sum of all four sides.

Test: 5 units × 5 units = 25 units, or 25 sq. m.

To cover the greatest possible area, Gwynne's garden should be 5 meters by 5 meters.

1. For a mural contest, each finalist will get a wall area of 12 square meters. Whoever figures out the greatest perimeter for that area will get first choice of wall space. What perimeter did the winner choose?

Think of numbers that can be multiplied to make 12. Then add these numbers together. Use graph paper to help you.

Your first guess:
Length: 3 Width: 4
(because 3 × 4 = 12)
Add 3 + 3 + 4 + 4

Perimeter: _____ m

Your second guess:
Length: 6 Width: 2
(because 6 × 2 = 12)
Add 6 + 6 + 2 + 2

Perimeter: _____ m

Your third guess:

Length: 12 Width: 1
(because 12 × 1 = 12)
Add 12 + 12 + 1 + 1

Perimeter: _____ m

The perimeter the winner chose:

_____

Exercises

Use guess and test to solve.

2. Find the greatest perimeter for a yard with an area of 72 square meters.

_____

3. A box of 36 chocolate tiles has a perimeter of 24 tiles. What is the box's length and width in tiles?

_____

Application

4. Suppose you are given an area and want to create a rectangle with the greatest possible perimeter. What rule could you make about the length and width of the rectangle that would give the greatest perimeter?

_____

USE ESTIMATION

Problem 1

The baseball team holds a spaghetti dinner to raise money for charity. Dennis is in charge of buying the milk and soda for the dinner. Last year they used 402 cartons of milk and 336 cans of soda. This year the team sold about the same number of tickets as last year. How many of each drink should Dennis order this year?

Make a plan.

Dennis estimates to determine an answer. To make sure he has enough for everyone, he decides to overestimate.

Carry out the plan.

He overestimates by rounding up the numbers of drinks.

$$402 \longrightarrow 450 \qquad 336 \longrightarrow 350$$

So Dennis orders 450 cartons of milk and 350 cans of soda.

Problem 2

The money raised from the team's dinner is donated to a local charity organization. Last year the team donated $853, the year before that they gave $812, and the year before that they gave $929. Mrs. Patel, the director of the charity, is planning her yearly budget. She needs to estimate how much the team will donate. About how much should she expect?

Make a plan.

Mrs. Patel doesn't want to base her budget plan on an unrealistically high amount. To arrive at a more realistic number, she uses underestimation.

Carry out the plan.

She underestimates by taking the least amount the team has donated in the past three years and rounding down.

$$\$812 \longrightarrow \$800$$

Mrs. Patel can expect at least $800 from the team.

Once you estimate, you can add, subtract, multiply, or divide with your rounded numbers.

1. Zeke is estimating how much money his students' group can donate to the charity organization. Last year they made $275 selling T-shirts and $578 from a white elephant sale. How much might they be able to donate this year if they raise about the same amount?

   a. Should Zeke overestimate or underestimate?

   b. About how much might the team be able to donate?

   Round: $275 ⟶ $_____ $578 ⟶ $_____

   Add the rounded amounts:

   $_____ + $_____ = $_____

Exercises

Use estimation to solve. Tell whether you used overestimation or underestimation.

2. To bake pastries for the charity dinner, Rae Ann will need 4 pounds of butter. Butter will cost her $1.89 a pound. Estimate how much Rae Ann will pay for butter.

   _____

3. At last year's baseball championship, attendance included 246 adults, 433 teenagers, and 328 children. The league's organizers are trying to estimate their ticket sales for this year's championship. About how many people should the organizers expect this year?

   _____

Application

COOPERATIVE
LEARNING

4. Work in groups of 3 or 4 to plan a class party. Consider what foods or drinks you would have. Estimate how much you would have to order and what you would have to spend. Then estimate how much money you could raise to pay for the party. Explain your methods below.

   _____

   _____

WORK BACKWARD

Jeff paid $10,000 for a car. Taxes were $1,000. Freight was $800. The dealer made a profit of $500. What did the dealer originally pay for the car?

What do you need to find?
You need to find what the dealer paid for the car.

Make a plan.
You can work backward to solve this problem. Use a calculator to help you subtract.

Try the plan.
Start at $10,000, the price Jeff paid for the car. Work backward by subtracting.

Subtract $1,000 for taxes.

$$\$10,000 - \$1,000 = \$9,000$$

Subtract $800 for freight.

$$\$9,000 - \$800 = \$8,200$$

Subtract $500 for the dealer's profit.

$$\$8,200 - \$500 = \$7,700$$

The dealer's original cost was $7,700.

Look back. Have you answered the question? Is the solution reasonable?
Yes, I found the dealer's original cost, $7,700. The solution is less than $10,000 (the price of the car altogether), so it seems reasonable.

Guided Practice

1. Sharla got to school at 8:00 A.M. today. It takes 5 minutes by car to get from her home to the school. On the way she stopped for breakfast (15 minutes) and to pick up a friend (10 minutes). What time did she leave home?

   Begin with the time Sharla arrived at school. Work backward.

   8:00 A.M. $\longrightarrow$ subtract 5 minutes $\longrightarrow$ 7:55 A.M.
   7:55 A.M. $\longrightarrow$ subtract 15 minutes $\longrightarrow$ 7:40 A.M.
   7:40 A.M. $\longrightarrow$ subtract 10 minutes

   $\longrightarrow$ _____ A.M.

   Sharla left home at _____ A.M.

Work backward to solve the problem. Use a calculator if necessary.

2. The owner of a hardware store sells a hammer for $9.99. She makes a profit of $1.00. The wholesaler that she buys from makes a profit of $1.50. How much does the hammer cost the wholesaler?

_____

3. Malik needs to get to basketball practice at 4:30. It takes 12 minutes to walk to the gym. He needs to stop at the store for his mother (10 minutes) and pick up his friend Bob (5 minutes). What time should he leave his house?

_____

4. A restaurant sells a hamburger for $1.00. Labor costs are 10¢ per hamburger. The meat costs 45¢, and the bread costs 10¢. Other costs add up to 15¢. What is the restaurant's profit on each hamburger?

_____

Application

5. Write a description of how you spent your time this morning. Now write a problem about your morning that could be solved using the work backward strategy.

_____

_____

_____

_____

_____

_____

_____

_____

BREAK A PROBLEM INTO SMALLER PARTS

Sam's mom wants him to varnish the wood floors in the kitchen and family room. He has these measurements.

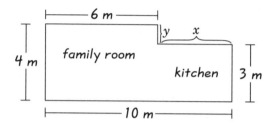

How can Sam find out the area of the wood floors so that he can buy enough varnish?

Sam breaks the problem into smaller parts.

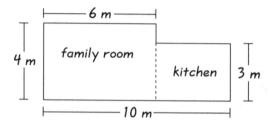

He draws an imaginary line between the rooms. This creates two rectangles. First, he will find the length and width of each rectangle. Then he can find the area of each rectangle.

The combined length of both rooms is 10 m.
The length of the family room is 6 m.
The length of the kitchen is unknown. Sam uses x to stand for this number.

$$x = 10 - 6, \text{ or } 4.$$

The kitchen is 3 m wide.
One end of the family room is 4 m wide.
The other end is 3 m plus an unknown small amount.
Sam uses y to stand for this unknown small amount.

$$y = 4 - 3, \text{ or } 1.$$

Now Sam can find the area of each room.

Area of family room   Area of kitchen

$4 \times 6 = 24$ sq. m $3 \times 4 = 12$ sq. m

Reminder

Area is the number of square units needed to cover a region. Perimeter is the distance around a figure.

Reminder

Manipulatives or diagrams can help you solve problems involving area and perimeter.

Reminder

The opposite sides of a rectangle are the same length.

Sam adds the two areas together.

$$24 \text{ sq. m} + 12 \text{ sq. m} = 36 \text{ sq. m}$$

Sam needs enough varnish to cover 36 square meters.

Guided Practice

1. Sam must buy painter's tape to protect the baseboards in both rooms. To find out how much tape he needs, he must find the perimeter around the outside of the two rooms. Remember—there is no baseboard along the imaginary line between the two rooms. So Sam won't use the measurements of the two rectangles as he did before.

   Step 1: Remember that you already know x and y for these two rooms.

   $x = $ _____ $y = $ _____

   Step 2: Add all the outside measurements. Use the drawing to help you.

   _____ + _____ + _____ + _____

   + _____ + _____ = _____

Sam must buy enough tape to protect _____ meters of baseboard.

Exercises

Break the problems into smaller parts and solve.

2. What is the perimeter of the closet? _____

3. What is the perimeter of the shape that is formed by the two rooms? _____

4. What is the total area of the two rooms? _____

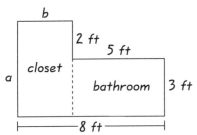

Application

COOPERATIVE LEARNING **Work with a partner. Use a measuring tape or ruler.**

5. Estimate the total area of two walls in your classroom. Do not include the area taken up by doors and windows.

_____

_____

DRAW A DIAGRAM

Dolores is a ticket agent for a railroad line. She is studying a train line that connects six cities.

- Two tracks connect to Arlington. One goes 9 miles west to Blair, and one goes 10 miles southwest to Sandtown.
- One track goes 8 miles south from Blair to Sandtown.
- One track goes 8 miles southwest from Sandtown to Raritan, and another track goes 10 miles southeast from Sandtown to Newark.
- A train track goes 10 miles east from Mesa to Blair and 9 miles south from Mesa to Raritan.

What routes can Dolores suggest for a passenger traveling from Mesa to Newark? Which route should she recommend?

Plan your strategy.
One way to solve the problem is to draw a diagram and then trace the routes. Then figure the mileage for each route.

Carry out your plan.
Here is one route Dolores could suggest.

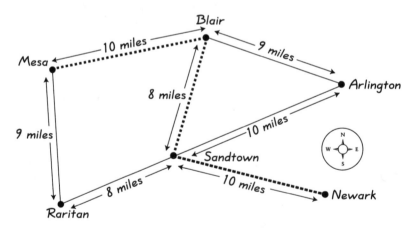

Suggested route:

10 miles + 8 miles + 10 miles = 28 miles

1. a. Another possible route is from Mesa to Blair to Arlington to Sandtown, and then on to Newark. Trace the route on the diagram. How many miles would the passenger travel?

_____

b. Find a third possible route from Mesa to Newark. Show the route in a different color. How many miles would the passenger travel?

_____

c. Dolores will recommend the shortest route. Which route is that?

_____

Exercises

Draw a diagram to solve. For each answer, give the names of the towns or cities.

2. Bus routes connect these towns:
- from Bel Air northeast to Havre de Grace (15 miles)
- from Havre de Grace south to Aberdeen (6 miles)
- from Aberdeen west to Bel Air (10 miles)
- from Bel Air south to Fallston (5 miles)
- from Bel Air west to Jarrettsville (7 miles)

a. What is the shortest route from Jarrettsville to Havre de Grace?

_____

b. What is the shortest route from Fallston to Aberdeen?

_____

c. Suppose the road from Bel Air to Aberdeen closed for repairs. What would then be the shortest route from Fallston to Aberdeen?

_____

Application

3. Use a map of a state of your choice. Find the shortest route by car from any location to another location at least 100 miles away. Trace the route with your finger or a pencil. Draw or describe the route.

_____

Vocabulary

table: an orderly arrangement of facts or information

graph: a method of presenting information using points, bars, lines, or pictures

Reminder

A percentile is a ranking based on percent. People in the 99th percentile of a group do better than 99% of the group. Those people are in the top 1% of the group—the highest rank.

USE A TABLE OR GRAPH

Tables

A physical fitness expert recorded how many chin-ups in a row boys and girls could do. Here is how the boys scored:

Number of Chin-Ups by Age (Boys)

Age	12	13	14	15	16
99th percentile	13	17	18	18	20
50th percentile	3	4	5	7	9
25th percentile	0	1	2	4	6

You can use a table to solve problems. The information on a table can help you answer questions, make comparisons, and draw conclusions.

Answering a question: How many chin-ups could the top 14-year-olds do?

> *Since those in the 99th percentile scored the best, find the row labeled "99th percentile." Then move along the row until you find the column for those aged 14.*

The answer is 18 chin-ups.

Making a comparison: How many more chin-ups could a 16-year-old in the 25th percentile do than a 12-year-old in the same percentile?

> *Find each group on the table.*
>
> > *The 16-year-olds did 6 chin-ups.*
> >
> > *The 12-year-olds did 0 chin-ups.*
>
> *Then subtract: 6 - 0 = 6*

So the 16-year-olds did 6 more chin-ups.

Drawing a conclusion: What can you conclude about how strength changes as boys grow?

You can conclude that as boys get older, they get stronger. You can make this conclusion because in every percentile, the number of chin-ups boys can do gets greater as they get older.

Sometimes a table does not contain enough information to answer a question. For example, this table cannot help you determine how many chin-ups boys in the 80th percentile did.

Graphs

A graph can also be used to solve problems.

The fitness expert made this double-bar graph to show how high a group of top student athletes jumped. Like a table, a graph can be used to answer questions, compare data, and draw conclusions.

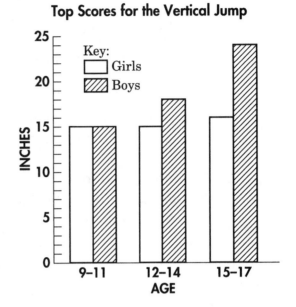

Top Scores for the Vertical Jump

Answering a question: How high did the top 14-year-old girls jump?

Use the key to determine which bars show data about girls. Find the bar on the graph that represents 12- to 14-year-old girls. Follow along the graph to see what inch mark the bar reaches.

The 14-year-old girls jumped 15 inches.

Making a comparison: How much higher did 15-year-old girls jump than 12-year-old girls?

Find the two bars that give the data that will be compared. Determine how high each of these bars reaches. Then subtract.

16 – 15 = 1

The older girls jumped 1 inch higher.

Drawing a conclusion: What can you conclude about the height that boys and girls can jump as they grow?

One conclusion you can make is that as boys and girls grow, boys can jump higher than girls.

Not enough information: Just as with a table, a graph may not contain enough information to answer certain questions. For example, you cannot tell from this graph how high 18-year-old boys can jump.

Use the table on page 24 for Problems 1 and 2.

1. How many more chin-ups did 12-year-old boys in the 99th percentile do than 12-year-old boys in the 50th percentile?

   a. The information is in the rows labeled _____ percentile and

   _____ percentile.

   b. The information is in the column labeled _____.

   c. Boys in the 99th percentile did _____ more chin-ups than those in the 50th percentile.

2. Use information from the table to think about a. and b. If you can make the conclusion that is presented, answer the question. Otherwise, write "not enough information."

   a. Do most boys stay in the same percentile as they get older?

   _____

   b. Are most boys able to do more chin-ups as they get older?

   _____

Use the graph on page 25 for Problems 3–5.

3. How much higher did 13-year-old boys jump than 13-year-old girls?

   a. To answer, compare the two bars labeled

   _____

   b. 13-year-old boys jumped _____ inches higher than 13-year-old girls.

4. Use information from the graph to think about a. and b. If you can make the conclusion that is presented, answer the question. Otherwise, write "not enough information."

   a. Is there any age at which boys and girls might be able to compete against one another fairly in sports meets?

   _____

   b. Do 7-year-old girls have equal, greater, or less jumping skill than 7-year-old boys?

   _____

Use the table to solve Exercises 5 and 6.

5. How far should a girl try to cycle each day the first week?

_____ miles

6. In how much time should a boy cycle 5 miles the third week?

_____ minutes

Bicycling Program for Age 14 to 18			
Week	Distance (miles per day)	Goal (in minutes)	
		Girls	Boys
1	5	30	28
2	5	28	25
3	5	27	23
4	6	34	26
5	6	30	24

To read a line graph, see where each dot is placed. The dot for Week 1 is at the $\frac{1}{2}$ mile mark. Callie ran $\frac{1}{2}$ mile that week.

7. How far did Callie run the second week?

_____ miles

8. In what weeks did Callie run the same mileage as she ran the week before?

Weeks _____

and _____

and _____ and _____

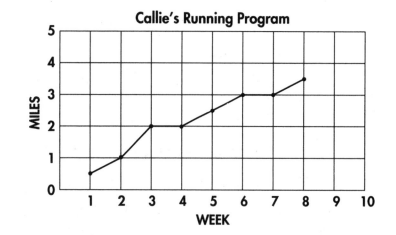

Callie's Running Program

9. Find a graph or table in a newspaper or magazine or elsewhere. Write a problem that can be solved using the graph or table.

_____

_____

MAKE A TABLE

Ved and Luis both began work on the same day. Ved's starting salary was $17,000 a year, while Luis's was $15,500. Each year Ved got a raise of $500 a year, while Luis got a raise of $1,000. Who made the higher salary in the fifth year?

One way to solve this problem is to make a table.

Step 1
Make a row to show each year. Divide the rows into columns, one column for each year.

Year	1	2	3	4	5

Step 2
Make a row to show each man's salary. Write the first year's salary in the first row, since this information is given in the problem.

Year	1	2	3	4	5
Ved	$17,000				
Luis	$15,500				

Step 3
Fill in the rows to show Ved's salary. For Year 2, add $500 to $17,000. For Year 3, add $500 to Year 2's salary, and so on. Use a calculator if you wish.

Year	1	2	3	4	5
Ved	$17,000	$17,500	$18,000	$18,500	$19,000
Luis	$15,500				

Step 4
To find Luis's salary, add $1,000 for each year.

Year	1	2	3	4	5
Ved	$17,000	$17,500	$18,000	$18,500	$19,000
Luis	$15,500	$16,500	$17,500	$18,500	$19,500

The table shows that Luis made more than Ved in the fifth year.

1. Terri has been offered two jobs. One pays $5.25 an hour. Every 6 months she will receive a $0.50 per hour raise. The other pays $5.75 an hour. Every 6 months she will receive $0.25 an hour more. Make a table to find which job will pay her more per hour after 2 years (24 months).

Finish the table to solve the problem.

Month	6	12	18	24
Job 1	$5.25	$5.75		
Job 2	$5.75	$6.00		

Exercises

Make a table to solve. Use a calculator if necessary.

2. Erica and Angela began work on the same day. Erica started at $13,000 a year, while Angela started at $12,000. Each year Erica got a raise of $500 a year, while Angela got a raise of $750 a year. Who made the

higher salary in the fourth year? _____

Year				
Erica				
Angela				

3. Two workers in a telephone sales department start work on a Monday. Sari calls 50 customers the first day. Each day after that she calls 5 more customers than the day before. (So she calls 60 customers on Wednesday, for instance.) Karen calls 53 customers the first day. Each day after that she calls 4 more customers than the day before. Which

salesperson calls more customers on Friday? _____

Application

COOPERATIVE
LEARNING

4. Work with a partner to find out what 3 local jobs pay. Ask the owner or manager what raises the average worker might expect during the first year. If you cannot find such information, make up three sets of data among yourselves. Then make a table to show which job offers the best pay after a certain period of time.

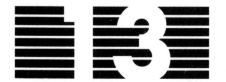

MAKE AN ORGANIZED LIST

Reminder

Manipulatives can help you solve problems. Try using a different-colored cube or slip of paper to stand for each boy on the team. Arrange the cubes or papers in different combinations. Record each combination on your list.

Coach Franklin has 6 players on his basketball team. Only 5 boys can play at a time. How many possible choices does the coach have for a 5-player team?

| John |
| Keith |
| Latik |
| Mike |
| Nick |
| Oscar |

Plan.

You can solve this problem by making an organized list of each possible team. List the boys by their first initials. Include all possibilities, with no repeats.

Carry out your plan.

First, list all the possibilities with John. These possibilities include a combination without Keith, one without Latik, one without Mike, one without Nick, and one without Oscar.

| JLMNO |
| JKMNO |
| JKLNO |
| JKLMO |
| JKLMN |

Then list all the possibilities without John:

KLMNO

There are no other possibilities without repeating.

Look back.

To prove to yourself that there are no other possibilities without repeating, try listing a team that includes Latik but not Keith.

The team would have to include John: LMNOJ

Since this is the same team as JLMNO, it is not a new possibility.

As you try other combinations, you will find that they also repeat. Therefore, all possibilities have been found.

Coach Franklin can form 6 5-man teams.

Guided Practice

1. Jules can play only 3 songs on his radio show today. He has a list of 6 favorite songs. What possible 3-song combinations can he play? (Use a letter from A to F for each song title.)

A _____, A _____, A _____, A _____, A _____,

A _____, A _____, A _____, A _____, B _____,

B _____, B _____, B _____, B _____, B _____,

C _____, C _____, C _____, D _____,

Exercises

Make an organized list to solve.

2. Remember that Jules has 6 songs: A, B, C, D, E, and F. Suppose he decides to play songs A and B plus 2 of the other songs—4 songs in all. What combinations could he play?

_____

_____

3. Mission Control is planning to choose the next space shuttle crew from these 5 astronauts: Lee, Ravenna, Graciela, Yuki, and Manuel

a. What possible choices does Mission Control have for a 4-person crew?

_____

_____

_____

b. Ravenna is being considered as captain for a 3-person crew. What possible choices would include her in a 3-person crew?

_____

_____

_____

c. What if Yuki becomes ill and can't go on the mission? What possible choices would Mission Control have for a 3-person crew?

_____

Application

4. Describe how to set up an organized list.

_____

_____

FIND A PATTERN

Reminder
You can draw a picture to help you see this pattern.

Reminder
To check your answer, use one of the methods you didn't use to solve the problem.

For a banquet in a gym, the caterer pushes small tables together to make a long table. Each small table seats 4 people. The gym can fit a long table made of 19 small tables pushed together. How many seats is that?

One way to solve this problem is to find a pattern.

A single table fits 4 seats.

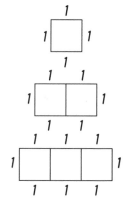

Pushing 2 tables together gives 6 places for people to sit:

Pushing 3 tables together gives 8 places for people to sit:

To find the pattern, the caterer creates a table or chart. This helps her keep track of the numbers.

Number of Tables	Number of Seats
1	4
2	6
3	8
4	10

The caterer finds 3 patterns:

Pattern A:
- Each added table increases the seats by 2.

Pattern B:
- 4 people fit at 1 table: 4 − 1 = 3
- 6 people fit at 2 tables: 6 − 2 = 4
- 8 people fit at 3 tables: 8 − 3 = 5
- 10 people fit at 4 tables: 10 − 4 = 6

The difference between the number of seats and the number of tables goes up 1 each time.

Pattern C: (Look back at the pictures to help you.)
This pattern starts *after* 1 table.
- 2 tables fit 2 people on each side and 1 at each end
- 3 tables fit 3 people on each side and 1 at each end
- 4 tables fit 4 people on each side and 1 at each end

Each time the total is 2 times (double) the number of tables, plus 2 (1 at each end).

$$2 \times 2 + 2 = 6 \qquad\qquad 3 \times 2 + 2 = 8$$
$$4 \times 2 + 2 = 10 \qquad\qquad 5 \times 2 + 2 = ?$$

Now you can solve the problem in several ways.
- Continue the table until you reach 19.
- Use Pattern A or B to count up to your answer. You could still use the table to keep track of the numbers.
- Use Pattern C: $19 \times 2 = 38$ $\qquad$ $38 + 2 = 40$

There will be 40 seats at a row of 19 connected tables.

Guided Practice

1. At one banquet, the caterer allows 3 desserts for every 2 people. How many desserts must the caterer prepare for 24 people?

Finish the table to find the pattern.

People:	2	4	6	8	10	12	14	16	18	20	22	24
Desserts:	3	6	9	12								

_____ desserts

Exercises

Complete the table and solve.

2. a. Bus fare in one county is $.30 for every 6 miles you travel. What is the fare for 36 miles?

$ _____

Fare	$0.30	$0.60	$0.90			
Miles	6	12				

Application

COOPERATIVE
LEARNING

3. A number multiplied by itself equals a *square number*. Thus, 1 squared (or 1×1) is 1; 2 squared is 4, 3 squared is 9, and 4 squared is 16. Work with a partner. Use a table to figure out the pattern of how square numbers such as 1, 4, 9, and so on change. Then, *without multiplying,* figure out what the square number after 64 will be.

MAKE A GENERALIZATION

Vocabulary

interior angles: the inside angles of a figure

polygon: a closed plane figure formed by line segments—for example, a triangle, a square, or a hexagon

generalization: a rule or conclusion you can make based on particular facts or observations

quadrilateral: any 4-sided polygon such as a square, a rectangle, a parallelogram, or a trapezoid

Reminder

Some problems can be solved by finding a pattern. To organize the information, it helps to make a table.

Suppose you wish to find the sum of the **interior angles**, or inside angles, of an octagon. An octagon is a **polygon** with eight sides and eight angles. How could you find out without measuring the angles and adding them up?

One way is to look at other polygons with a smaller number of interior angles and then make a **generalization**, or rule, based on your observations.

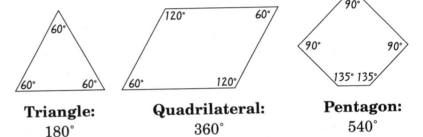

| **Triangle:** 180° | **Quadrilateral:** 360° | **Pentagon:** 540° |

To find the pattern, make a table.

Polygon	Number of Sides	Sum of Interior Angles
triangle	3	180°
quadrilateral	4	360°
pentagon	5	540°

Here is one way to describe the pattern:
Add 180° for each additional side.

You can use a calculator to find the sum of the interior angles of a hexagon, heptagon, and octagon.

Polygon	Number of Sides	Sum of Interior Angles
hexagon	6	720°
heptagon	7	900°
octagon	8	1,080°

Guided Practice

1. You can divide a quadrilateral into 2 triangles. You can divide a hexagon into 4 triangles. How many triangles can you draw in an octagon?

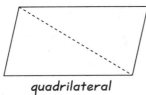
quadrilateral

hexagon

a. Fill in the table. You can draw diagrams to help you.

Polygon	Number of Sides	Number of Triangles
triangle	3	1
quadrilateral	4	2
pentagon	5	
hexagon	6	4
heptagon		
octagon		

b. What generalization can you make from the table?

_____

Exercises

Fill in the table below. Also make diagrams to help you.

2. The diagonal of a polygon is a line segment other than a side that joins any 2 angles. In a pentagon you can draw 5 diagonals. How many diagonals can be drawn in a

hexagon? _____

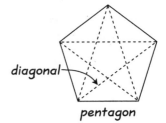
diagonal
pentagon

3. How many diagonals can be drawn in a heptagon? _____

Polygon	Number of Sides	Number of Diagonals
triangle	3	0
quadrilateral	4	2
pentagon	5	5
hexagon		
heptagon		

Application

COOPERATIVE
LEARNING

4. Work with a small group. Compare the number of triangles into which you can divide a polygon to the sum of the interior angles. What generalization can you make?

SOLVE A SIMPLER PROBLEM

Reminder

Imagine a number line of all the numbers from 1 to 100 in order. Notice that you always pick numbers from opposite ends of the line. The numbers of the last pair "meet" in the middle—50 and 51.

Reminder

Before making a generalization, solve several problems to make sure that the rule holds true. In this case, add several pairs of numbers from 1 to 100. You won't have to add every pair to confirm the rule, though.

Can you find the sum of all the whole numbers from 1 to 100 without adding them all up? You can if you use this shortcut: solve a simpler problem.

Add pairs of numbers from each end of the range of 1 and 100. Never use the same numbers twice.

$$1 + 100 = 101 \qquad 49 + 52 = 101$$
$$2 + 99 = 101 \qquad 50 + 51 = 101$$

There are 50 combinations of numbers adding up to 101, so you multiply 101 by 50.

$$101 \times 50 = 5,050 \qquad \text{The correct solution is 5,050.}$$

You can use shortcuts to solve many kinds of problems.

A state with 300 schools will play a "single elimination" basketball tournament—one loss and you're out. How many games must be played to determine a champion?

Solve several simpler problems.

How many games would 6 schools play?

Round 1 would have 3 games. Each game would have 1 winner. The 3 winning teams would advance to Round 2. Round 2 would consist of 1 game between 2 of the remaining teams. In Round 3 the winner of that game would play the other remaining team.

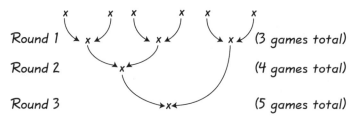

So 6 schools must play 5 games.

Find out how many games 8 schools would play.

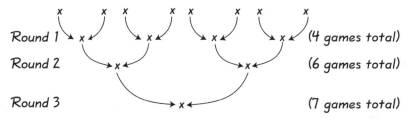

So 8 schools must play 7 games to determine a champion.

Make a generalization based on the simpler problems.
You can conclude that the teams play 1 less game than the total number of teams. So 300 teams must play 299 games.

Guided Practice

1. What is the average of the sum of all the whole numbers from 1 through 100?

   a. Solve simpler problems.
   First find the average of the numbers 1 through 7.
   Add the numbers on a calculator:

   $1 + 2 + 3 + 4 + 5 + 6 + 7 =$ _____

   Divide that number by the total amount of numbers:

   $28 \div 7 =$ _____

   So _____ is the average of the numbers 1 through 7.

   Then find the average of the numbers from 1 through 10.
   Add and then divide.

   $1 + 2 + 3 + 4 + 5 + 6 + 7 + 8 + 9 + 10 =$ _____

   $55 \div 10 =$ _____

   So _____ is the average of the numbers 1 through 10.

   b. Make a generalization.
   The average of the numbers is the number found

   _____ between 1 and the last number.

Exercises

Use a simpler problem to solve. You can use a calculator or write out a number line to help you.

2. What is the sum of all whole numbers from 1 to 50? _____

3. What is the average of numbers from 1 through 50? _____

Application

COOPERATIVE
LEARNING

4. Work with a partner to solve this problem. At a party, 26 people walk into a room, one at a time. On walking in, each person shakes hands with everyone in the room. Thus, the first person shakes hands 0 times, the second person shakes hands 1 time, and so on. How many times does the 26th person shake hands?

SOLVE ANOTHER WAY

Gus and Makal play center for the Ravens, a basketball team. For the next 3 games, how many different possibilities are there for who will start as center?

Plan your strategy.
You can use at least two different strategies to solve this problem: Make An Organized List and Use Manipulatives.

Recall that to make an organized list, you can list the players by their first initials. Include all possibilities, with no repeats.

Organized List	
GGG	MMM
GMM	MGG
GGM	MMG
GMG	MGM

There are 8 possible ways that the manager could start the 2 centers.

To use manipulatives, use pennies to stand for Gus and dimes to stand for Makal.

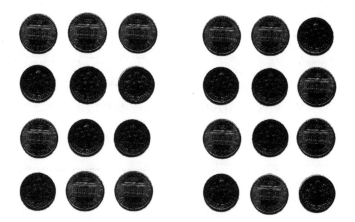

This method gives the same answer.

Look back.
One reason to use two different strategies is to confirm your answer. Both the organized list and the manipulatives show that the manager has 8 ways to start the 2 centers in the next 3 basketball games.

Guided Practice

1. A cashier started work with some money in the cash box. Then she rang up sales of $55, $35, and $20. When she counted the money in the cash box, she had $150. How much money did she begin with?

You can try two different strategies to solve this problem: Work Backward or Guess and Test.

a. First try Guess and Test. Add with a calculator.
First guess: the cashier began with $25 in the cash box.

$25 + $55 + $35 + $20 = _____

This guess is too low because it is _____ than $150.

Second guess: the cashier began with $40 in the cash box.

$40 + _____ + _____ + _____ = _____

This guess is _____.

b. Confirm your answer with Work Backward. Use a calculator.

$150 − $20 − $35 − $55 = _____

c. How much money did the cashier begin with? _____

Exercises

Use one strategy to solve. Then use a different strategy to confirm your answer.

2. Mary sells 3 kinds of souvenirs: a cup, a flag, and a T-shirt. She will display them in a row with one at each end and one in the middle. How many different ways can she set up the row?

First strategy: _____

Second strategy: _____

3. Diana left the arena at sunset. She walked along the river for 10 minutes, then stopped for a snack for 25 minutes. Then she walked another 10 minutes. She arrived home at 7:55. What time was sunset?

First strategy: _____

Second strategy: _____

Application

COOPERATIVE
LEARNING

4. Discuss this situation with your group. Suppose you need to measure something to solve a problem. However, you don't have a ruler or tape measure. What could you do as an alternate strategy? Give several specific examples of situations.

Vocabulary

sample: a small part of a group that shows the characteristics of the entire group

Reminder

You can use estimation to solve a problem.

Reminder

If a more accurate estimate is needed, Sal might take several samples. He would use an average number from those samples for his multiplication.

USE A SAMPLE

Sal works at City Park. Today there is a free concert at the park. Park officials want to know how many people attend the concert. How can Sal give a reasonable estimate of the number of people?

One way is to use a **sample**, or small part of the group, to estimate how many are in the whole group.

To take a sample, Sal counts how many people are in a small area.

The x's stand for the people he counts in an area about 25 ft by 20 ft.

```
┌─────────────────────────┐
│  XX  X  XXX  X  X  X     │
│      X  X  XX  X         │
│    X  XX  XXXX  XX       │
│   XX  XXX  XXXX  XX      │
└─────────────────────────┘
```

There are 34 people in this sample. Sal will use this sample to estimate.

Sam knows that the area where the concert is being held is about 100 ft by 100 ft. (But if he didn't know how large the area was, he could estimate that also.) The sample he took is 25 ft by 20 ft, so he divides the larger area into a grid of rectangles of that size.

From his sample, he estimates about 34 people in each rectangle.

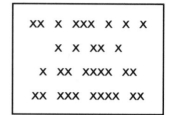

There are 20 rectangles of about 34 people.

$$20 \times 34 = 680$$

So there are about 680 people at the concert.

1. How could Sal estimate the number of squirrels in the park?

   a. He counts 15 squirrels in an area 100 m by 100 m.

   b. The entire park is about 800 m by 1,000 m. Use graph paper to make a grid that shows how many 100-m-by-100-m squares are in the park. Let each square on the graph paper stand for one 100-m-by-100-m square.

   There are _____ squares in the whole park.

   c. Use a calculator to multiply the number of squares times the number of squirrels in the sample:

   _____ × _____ = _____

   d. There are about _____ squirrels in the park.

Exercises

 Use a sample to solve. Use a calculator if necessary.

2. At a children's show at the same location the next week, Sal counts these people in a 25-ft-by-20-ft area at City Park. About how many people are at the show?

   _____

 3. Take a handful of coins. Let each kind of coin stand for a different kind of animal in a 100-m-by-100-m area of a park.

   a. Based on your sample, how many animals are there in a

   1,000-m-by-1,000-m area? _____

   b. How many of each kind of animal is in the 1,000-m-by-1,000-m area?

   _____

Application

4. Suppose you work for the City Park cafeteria. You want to find how many visitors buy snacks at the park in one day. How could you use a sample to make a reasonable estimate?

 _____

Vocabulary

Venn diagram: a graph that uses circles to show the relationship between two or more sets

set: a group or collection of elements

intersection: the set of elements common to two or more sets

Reminder

A graph is a visual way to represent data and to solve problems.

USE VENN DIAGRAMS

A supermarket survey of customers' favorite fruits found that 12 people preferred apples and 13 people preferred grapes. Yet only 20 surveys were filled out. This is because 5 customers listed both apples and grapes as their favorites.

Mrs. Velez, a customer, wanted to find out how many people listed *only* apples or *only* grapes as their favorites.

Make a plan.
Mrs. Velez drew a **Venn diagram.** This is a graph that uses circles to show the relationship between two or more groups of data. Mrs. Velez labeled one circle *apples* and the other circle *grapes*.

Carry out the plan.
Step 1 Mrs. Velez put a 5 at the **intersection** of the two circles. The 5 shows the **set**, or group, of people who chose both fruits as their favorites.

Step 2 In the survey, 12 people chose apples as their favorite fruits. Of these 12, 5 listed *both* apples and grapes. The rest listed apples *only*. Mrs. Velez subtracted to find out how many listed apples only.

$$12 - 5 = 7$$

Mrs. Velez put a 7 in the apples circle.

Step 3 In the survey, 13 people named grapes. Of these 13, 5 listed *both* apples and grapes. The rest listed grapes *only*. Mrs. Velez subtracted to find that number.

$$13 - 5 = 8$$

Mrs. Velez put an 8 in the grapes circle.

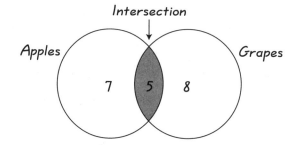

Look back. Does the answer seem reasonable?
Yes, because 7 + 5 + 8 = 20, the total number of people who filled out the survey.

1. When 50 customers voted on brands of soup, 20 people preferred the store brand and 25 preferred a national brand. In this group, 15 people liked both brands equally. The rest of the 50 customers didn't like either brand. How many people liked neither brand?

   a. Make a Venn diagram.

   b. Subtract to find how many people liked each brand only. Write these numbers in the correct circles.

   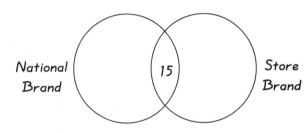

   National Brand   15   Store Brand

   20 − 15 = _____   25 − 15 = _____

   c. Add the numbers in the two circles and in the intersection.

   15 + _____ + _____ = _____

   d. Subtract that total from 50.   50 − _____ = _____

   _____ people liked neither brand.

Exercises

To solve, make a Venn diagram on another paper.

2. Danielle offered 60 shoppers a taste of blue cheese and a taste of cheddar cheese. Of these people, 35 sampled blue cheese and 30 tried cheddar. There were 27 who sampled both cheeses. How many people refused to taste either type of cheese?

   _____

Application

3. Use slips of different colored paper to sort data about the colors of clothing the members of your class are wearing. Create a large Venn diagram. The two circles on the Venn diagram will represent the clothing colors red and blue. Then sort the slips to show who is wearing red or blue, red and blue, or neither color. Explain your findings.

USE LOGICAL REASONING

Al, Ben, Carmen, and Delia each play a different sport—baseball, basketball, soccer, or volleyball.

Clue 1 Al does not play soccer.

Clue 2 Ben and Carmen saw the other girl play a volleyball match.

Clue 3 Carmen forgot her baseball uniform today.

Which sport does each person play?

Use logical reasoning to solve. The clues can help you. Organize the data in a table to keep track of it.

An X means "does not play this sport." For instance, you can figure out from Clue 3 that Carmen plays baseball. Write an X all the other boxes in her row, because she plays only baseball.

Also, every time you find out what one person plays, you know that no one else plays that sport. So write x for the baseball box in everyone's row except Carmen's.

	Baseball	Basketball	Soccer	Volleyball
Al	X		X	X
Ben	X	X		X
Carmen		X	X	X
Delia	X	X	X	

Conclusion: Al plays basketball, Ben plays soccer, Carmen plays baseball, and Delia plays volleyball.

Reminder

Tables can be used to organize information in an orderly, easy-to-use fashion. See Lessons 11 and 12, pages 24–29.

Reminder

Who is the other girl? If she plays volleyball, she doesn't play any other sport. That helps you fill in her entire row. Also, no one else plays volleyball. That helps you fill in the entire volleyball column.

Guided Practice

Reminder

What do the clues tell you about Ann? Think about the wording of the clues.

1. Ann, Jan, and Nan each like a different kind of pizza: either plain, with mushrooms, or with olives.

   - Ann doesn't know who likes her pizza plain.
   - Jan's favorite pizza is cheaper than pizza with olives.
   - The one who likes olives is Ann's cousin.

   Which girl likes her pizza plain?

   Complete the table. X means "does not like."

	Plain	Mushrooms	Olives
Ann	X		
Jan			
Nan			

Conclusion: _____ likes plain pizza.

Exercises

Use logical reasoning to solve.

2. Fred, Chris, and Brian play in a band trio made up of drums, a bass guitar, and a lead guitar. What instrument does each teenager play?

   • Fred does not play a stringed instrument.

   • Chris plays the bass guitar.

   a. Complete the table.

	Drums	Bass Guitar	Lead Guitar
Fred			
Chris			
Brian			

   b. Conclusion: Fred plays _____, Chris plays

   _____, and Brian plays _____.

3. Chad, Katrinka, Barbara, and Kyle each bought a different album on tape yesterday. The albums are called *Spin Dream*, *Call Me*, *School Song,* and *Beauty's Past*. What did each person buy yesterday?

   • Chad saw Barbara buying *Spin Dream*.
   • Katrinka and Kyle dislike the band who made *Beauty's Past*.
   • Kyle already bought *Call Me* two weeks ago.

   a. Make a table on another paper.

   b. Conclusion: _____

   _____

Application

COOPERATIVE
LEARNING

4. On another paper, write a problem that uses logical reasoning to solve. Then trade problems with another person and solve.

USE CRITICAL THINKING

Examine the following advertisement. Can you locate parts of it that present ideas in a misleading way?

Use critical thinking.

You've used critical thinking throughout this book to solve problems. A critical thinker examines several sides of a problem. A critical thinker might ask:

- What do I know about this problem?
- What do I want to know?
- Does the data make sense?
- Do my conclusions make sense?

When you examine an ad, ask questions such as these:

Are similar items being compared?

The prices look better at Hank's Bike Shop, but you need to find out if the boy's and girl's bikes being offered are the *same* bikes as those at the other bike shop.

Has the data in a graph or table been presented in a misleading way?

Look closely. Customers have increased only by 5 or 10 a month, but the graph has been constructed to make the growth in customers seem greater than that.

Who or what is the source of the advertisement?

Since the bike shop owners paid for the advertisement, of course they would say their service is best.

1. Use the advertisement to answer the questions.

   ALL-TERRAIN BIKES
   Final Cost **$129.99**
   $129.99 with trade-in bike. $149.99 without trade-in.

   a. How much does an all-terrain bike appear to cost if you glance at the ad quickly?

   _____

   b. How much does an all-terrain bike really cost unless you trade in your old bike? _____

Exercises

Use critical thinking to solve.

2. What is odd about this slogan?   **50% More People Shop Here!**

   _____

3. Look at the following graph. Why do you think the advertiser started the numbering at 10 million instead of at zero, the way graphs are usually set up?

   _____

   _____

   _____

   _____

   More People Choose Clean-On!

   Sales (in millions)

   12 — 11 — 10

   Clean-On   Best   Mildew-Off

Application

COOPERATIVE LEARNING

4. Work with a partner. Find several advertisements in a newspaper or magazine. Point out any misleading information. Then explain how you used critical thinking to evaluate the ads.

   _____

   _____

FIND THE BREAK-EVEN POINT

Vocabulary

revenue: money earned through sales of a product or service

break-even point: the point at which cost equals revenue

double-line graph: a diagram using lines to show the changes and relationships between two things

intersection: the point where the lines in a graph cross each other

Phil sells Frozen-Juice bars at his beach stand. A box of 10 juice bars costs Phil $6.00. He sells each bar for $1.00. The money he makes selling the bars is his **revenue**. What is Phil's **break-even point**, the point at which the bars' cost equals the revenue?

Phil uses a **double-line graph** to find the break-even point. The break-even point is at the **intersection** of the two lines, the point where they cross. On this graph it is at (6,6).

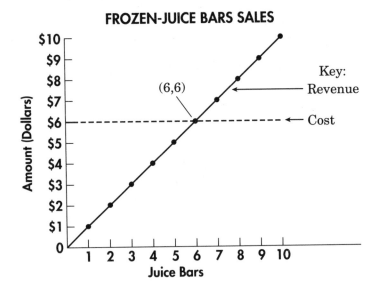

FROZEN-JUICE BARS SALES

The break-even point is 6 bars for $6, the point where the "cost" line crosses the "revenue" line. If Phil sells fewer than 6 bars, he will lose money. If he sells more than 6 bars he will make a profit.

Guided Practice

1. The line graph on the next page shows sales for a high school fundraiser. The dotted line reflects that the students pay a different amount per shirt depending on how many shirts they buy from the wholesaler. The more shirts they buy, the less they pay per shirt. If they buy 1 shirt, they pay $10. They pay $15 for 2 shirts, or $7.50 for each shirt. They decide to charge $5 for each shirt.

T-Shirt Sales

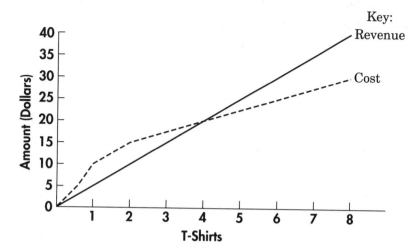

a. The lines on the graph intersect at (4, 20). This is the point where the students have paid _____ for the T-shirts.

b. How many T-shirts must be sold to break even? _____

Exercises

Use the Frozen-Juice Bars line graph to solve.

2. How much profit will Phil make if he sells 9 bars at $1 each? _____

3. Suppose Phil can buy a box of 10 bars for a reduced price of $4. He sells these bars for $1 each. How many bars must he sell to make a profit of $3? (Draw on the graph to help you.) _____

Use the T-shirt line graph to solve.

4. How many shirts must the students sell to make a profit of $10?

_____

5. How much profit will the students make if they sell 4 shirts at $10 a shirt instead of $5? _____

Application

COOPERATIVE

LEARNING

6. Work with a partner. On graph paper, copy the frame of the T-shirt graph from this lesson. Show what would happen if the students had to pay $30 for a box of 10 shirts and charged $5 for each shirt. With your partner, write two problems based on this graph.

WRITE AN EQUATION

Vocabulary

equation: a math sentence that shows equality between two quantities or expressions

variable: a quantity that can have any of a set of values; it is usually shown by a letter or a symbol

Reminder

Whatever you do to one side of an equation, you have to do to the other side, too. This keeps both sides equal in value.

On a recent trip, Tarathea's family drove 420 miles in 8 hours. What was their average speed per hour?

Use an equation.
To solve this problem, you can use the distance formula. The distance formula is an **equation**. In an equation, the numbers, or **variables**, on one side equal those on the other side.

distance = rate × time $d = r \times t$

Since you need to find the average speed per hour, or the rate, rewrite the equation to put r on one side by itself. To do that, you are dividing both sides of the equation by t.

$$\frac{d}{t} = r \times \frac{t}{t} \longrightarrow \frac{d}{t} = r$$

Then substitute the numbers that you know in place of the correct variables.

$$\frac{420}{8} = r$$

Use a calculator: $420 \div 8 = 52.5$

$$r = 52.5 \text{ miles per hour}$$

Tarathea's family's average speed was 52.5 miles per hour.

Guided Practice

1. Turk raced his bike around a track for 30 minutes at a speed of 12 miles per hour. How many miles did he bike?

   a. Use the distance formula to write an equation. Since the rate is written "per hour," write 30 minutes as 0.5 hour.

   $$d = \underline{\hspace{2cm}} \times 0.5$$

   b. Solve the equation. $d = \underline{\hspace{2cm}}$

   c. Turk biked \underline{\hspace{2cm}} miles.

Exercises

Write an equation to solve. Use a calculator when necessary.

2. Lila ran 4 miles in half an hour. What was her average running speed?

_____

3. Roland walked for 2 hours at a speed of 3 miles an hour. How far did he

walk? _____

4. In 1980, Jim King rode a roller coaster for 368 hours. He covered a distance of 10,425 miles. What was the average speed of the roller coaster? _____

5. The slowest moving land mammal is the sloth. Its average ground speed is 7 feet per minute. At that speed, how far can it travel in 5 minutes? _____

6. In short bursts of speed, a cheetah can run 60 miles per hour. At that rate, how long would it take a cheetah to run 15 miles?

_____

7. In 1978 Robert McGuiness rode a unicycle 3,976 miles across Canada in 79 days. How many miles per day did he ride?

_____

Application

8. How could you use the distance formula to find out how fast you ride a bike?

_____

_____

_____

_____

_____

_____

Use the four-step process to solve the problem.

1. What is the greatest odd number that contains the digits 2, 3, and 5?

_____

2. This number is greater than twice 17 and less than twice 21. It is an odd number and has 4 in the tens place. What is the number?

_____

Choose the correct operation or operations to solve the problem.

3. Elaine earns $226 each week. After 4 weeks, she bought a used car for

$850. How much money did she have left? _____

Decide what information you need to solve the problem. Then solve.

4. Cara had $100. She bought 3 shirts for $42 and 2 skirts for $38. How much did 1 shirt and 1 skirt cost? _____

Formulate and solve a problem based on the advertisement.

	Original Price	**SALE** Price
Sweaters	$32.50	$28.00
Jeans	$26.00	$22.00

5. Problem: _____

Solution: _____

6. Think about the four-step process. Write a question you might ask at each step of the process: Understand, Plan, Carry Out, and Look Back.

_____

_____

_____

Solve, using manipulatives and Guess and Test.

1. Vee is buying a pack of gum for 34¢. The 6 coins in her pocket add up to exactly the right change. What 6 coins are they?

_____

2. Cal wants to make a rectangle or square with a perimeter of 44 tiles and the greatest possible area. What will its length and width be?

_____

Use estimation to solve.

3. Annie needs about 4 pounds of chicken. Chicken costs $2.29 per pound. She is estimating how much money to take to the store.

   a. Should Annie overestimate or underestimate? _____

   b. About how much money will she need? _____

Work backward to solve.

4. Brad's car cost $11,500. Taxes were $750. Freight was $650. The dealer made a profit of $1,000. What was the dealer's original cost?

   _____

5. Courtney got home from school at 3:30. The walk home takes 6 minutes. On the way she stopped to buy school supplies for 15 minutes and talked to a friend (5 minutes). What time did she leave school?

   _____

Break the problem into smaller parts to solve.

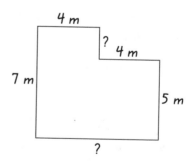

6. What is the perimeter of this figure?

   _____

7. What is the area of the figure?

   _____

8. What do you know about the size and shape of rectangles that helped you determine the answer to problems 6 and 7?

_____

10-13 CUMULATIVE REVIEW

Draw a diagram to solve.

1. Avenue A, which has been drawn for you, runs from east to west. Avenue B also runs from east to west. It is one block south of Avenue A. Street C runs north and south, connecting Avenues A and B. Street D runs parallel to Street C, one block east. How many routes can a person take to travel from the corner of Avenue A and Street C to the corner of Avenue B and Street D?

   Diagram: _____ Avenue A _____

   Solution: _____

Make a table to solve.

2. Roberta has been offered 2 jobs. One pays $6.00 an hour. Every year she will receive a raise of $1.00 per hour. The other job pays $5.75 an hour, and every year she will receive $1.50 an hour more. Finish the table to show how much she will be making after 4 years in each job.

Year				
Job 1				
Job 2				

Make an organized list to solve.

3. A program director has 3 spots open for performers on a special show. She has narrowed the list down to these 4 performers: Raphael, Bob, Jomo, and Tom. What possible choices does the director have for the order in which the performers will appear in the show? (Give each combination of names, not the number of combinations.)

_____

COOPERATIVE
LEARNING

4. Suppose Willie wants to record and compare the amount of time he spends watching TV every day for a week. Create a bar graph that shows Willie's TV watching time for seven days, Monday through Sunday. Then make up two problems that could be answered using information from your graph. Exchange problems with a friend. Evaluate and solve each other's problems.

Find a pattern to solve. Make a table to help you.

1. Each week, a swim team increases the daily distance that each member swims. The first week, members each swim 500 meters a day. The second week, they swim 600 meters. The third week, they each swim 725 meters, and the fourth week, they swim 875 meters. If the pattern continues, how many meters per day will they swim in Weeks 5 and 6?

   _____

   What generalization can you make based on the pattern you found?

   _____

2. The Richter scale measures the force of earthquakes. An earthquake measuring 2 on the scale is not twice as powerful but 10 times as powerful as an earthquake measuring 1. Complete the table to find the force of an earthquake measuring 7.

   What generalization can you make based on the table?

Richter Number	Increase in Force
1	1
2	10
3	
4	1000
5	
6	
7	

   _____

Use a simpler problem to solve.

3. Find the sum of all the whole numbers from 1 to 40. Explain your

   solution. _____

Solve using one strategy. Then check your answer by solving another way.

4. Dante spent $12.50 on snacks, $11.99 on a tape, $12 for movies, and $1.50 for library fines. He has $27.01 left. How much money did he

   have to begin with? _____

   First strategy: _____

   Second strategy: _____

5. Describe a problem situation in which Using Manipulatives and Making an Organized List could be used as alternative strategies to solve the problem. How could you use one strategy to check the other?

18-21 CUMULATIVE REVIEW

Use a sample to solve.

1. A rap group's manager counts this many people in a 20 ft by 20 ft area at a concert. The concert is taking place in a 40 ft by 80 ft area. About how many people are

   at the concert? _____

x x xx x x xxx
x xx x xx x xxx
x x xx x xxxx x x
x x x x xx xx x

`enn diagram to solve.

2. A radio announcer surveyed 50 people. He asked whether their favorite music was rap or rock. Of the people surveyed, 30 said they preferred rap, and 25 said they liked rock. Ten of these people said they liked both types of music equally well. How many liked neither kind of music?

   _____

Use logical reasoning to solve.

3. Francisco, Garth, and Henry all prefer different subjects at school. One boy likes math best. One likes science best. One likes English best.

   • Garth is good at math, but it's not his favorite subject.
   • Francisco wants to be a writer, so he works especially hard at his favorite subject.

	Math	Science	English
Francisco			
Garth			
Henry			

   What is each boy's favorite subject?

   _____

COOPERATIVE
LEARNING

4. Suppose you are writers for a consumer awareness magazine. Work together to come up with a set of tips for people to keep in mind when they look at ads for various products. These tips should make use of critical thinking skills you have learned and may be in the form of a magazine article.

Use the graph to solve.

1. How many plants must the class sell to break even?

_____

2. How much profit do they make if they sell 20 plants?

_____

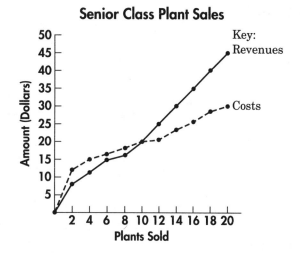

Senior Class Plant Sales

Key:
Revenues
Costs

Amount (Dollars)

Plants Sold

3. Explain how to find the break-even point on a double-line graph illustrating revenues and costs.

_____

_____

Write an equation to solve.

4. Jerilyn drove 350 miles in 7 hours. What was her average speed per hour? _____

5. Troy flew a plane at 450 miles per hour for 1 hour 30 minutes. How many miles did he travel? _____

6. Describe a way to check your answer when you are using the distance formula.

_____

_____

COOPERATIVE LEARNING

7. Work with your group to create problems about the area or perimeter of rectangles. Create equations to solve these problems. Then solve the problems. Use the following formulas:

$a = lw$ (the area equals the length times the width),

$l = \dfrac{a}{w}$ (the length equals the area divided by the width)

$p = 2l + 2w$ (the perimeter equals twice the length plus twice the width, or the sum of all 4 sides)

ANSWER KEY

LESSON 1 (pages 2–5)
1. a. I know that I can use the digits 3, 4, and 7 only once. I need to find out the least number I can make using those digits.
b. I can use the least digit in the hundreds place, the next least in the tens place, and the greatest in the ones place.
c. I'll make the number 347 with the three digits.
d. Yes, I made the least number I could with those three digits. Yes, the solution seems reasonable, because other numbers such as 437 or 374 are greater than 347.
3. a. I can use any three digits from 1 to 9. A digit may be used no more than twice.
b. I can use the greatest digit in the hundreds and tens places.
c. I'll form the number 998.
d. Yes, the answer is the greatest number I can make with those digits.
5. The number is between 2×30 and 2×35, which means it is between 60 and 70. Place a 6 in the ones place to get the solution: 66.
7. $5 = 1 hr.,
$10 = 2 hr.,
$15 = 3 hr.,
$20 = 4 hr.,
$25 = 5 hr.,
so Larome must work 5 hours to buy the $24 ticket.
9. Camilla had 6 cookies minus 2.
Camilla had 4 cookies minus 1.
Jack had 3 cookies minus 1, so he kept 2 cookies for himself.
11. Answers will vary.
Students can model their riddles on one of the riddles in the lesson.

LESSON 2 (pages 6–7)
1. $63 - 5 = 58$ people; $58 + 8 = 66$ people in all
3. subtraction, then addition; $7 - 2 = 5$ people; $5 + 3 = 8$ people in all
5. Answers will vary, but operations will probably include multiplication and addition.

LESSON 3 (pages 8–9)
1. Miguel's profit: $100 - $80 = $20
3. Necessary information:
How many shoes there are, what the assistant buyer paid for them this month, and what the store sells them for this year
Solution: $100 \times $75 = $7,500;
$7,500 - $4,000 = $3,500 total profit

5. Problems will vary, but they should contain extra information.

LESSON 4 (pages 10–11)
1. Answers will vary.
3–5. Sample problems:
How much will 5 copies of "Wild World" cost at the sale price?
Multiplication Sentence: $5 \times $28.79 = ?$
Solution: $5 \times $28.79 = 143.95
How much would 3 copies of Share Racer cost at the sale price?
Solution: $3 \times $59.99 = 179.97

LESSON 5 (PAGES 12–13)
1. 8 cars
3. 1 quarter + 2 dimes + 4 pennies
5. 1st floor
7. Possible answer:
Manipulatives help you to physically see the problem and keep track of changes.

LESSON 6 (pages 14–15)
1. Perimeter: 14 m;
Perimeter: 16 m;
Perimeter: 26 m;
The perimeter the winner chose: 26 m
3. Length: 6 units;
Width: 6 units

LESSON 7 (pages 16–17)
Note: Some students may round differently: for example, to the nearest 50 instead of the nearest 100. Accept reasonable answer variations based on different rounded numbers.
1. a. underestimate
b. $200 + 500 = $700;
the team should be able to donate at least $700.
3. Accept overestimate or underestimate.
Overestimate: 250 + 350 + 450 = 1,050 **people**;
underestimate: 200 + 300 + 400 = 900 people

LESSON 8 (pages 18–19)
1. Sharla left home at 7:30 A.M.
3. 4:30 → subtract 12 minutes → 4:18 → subtract 10 minutes → 4:08 → subtract 5 minutes → 4:03;
So he should leave his house at 4:03.
5. Answers will vary.

LESSON 9 (pages 20–21)
1. Step 1: $x = 4$ m ; $y = 1$ m;
Step 2: 4 m + 6 m + 1 m + 4 m + 3 m + 10 m = 28 m; Sam must buy enough tape to protect 28 meters of baseboard.